KING DESIG

Some Mothers Do 'Ave 'Em

Edited
By
ADAM KING

PUBLISHING

First published in Great Britain in 1997 by
KING DESIGNS
56 Bringhurst, Orton Goldhay,
Peterborough, PE2 5RT.

British Library Cataloguing in Publication Data.
A catalogue record for this book is available from the British Library.

Cover Design by Lyndsey Ramm

Printed and Bound in Great Britain by
Parrot Print Ltd
Unit 1 Park Farm Workshops,
Wood Lane, Ramsey,
Cambridgeshire, PE17 1XF.

Softback ISBN - 1 901349 02 0
Hardback ISBN - 1 901349 03 9

Foreword

For most people having a baby is the greatest event in their life!
This is the feeling that is expressed in the poems in this book. Love and
affection between parents and their babies can be the most wonderful
thing. Some Mother Do 'Ave 'Em celebrates this relationship, covering a
wide spectrum of emotions: passion; affection; laughter and sorrow all
playing their part.
Each poem will leave the reader to ponder over the power of love between
parents and their children.

Many thanks to the publishers who supported us through publicity -
Baby Magazine, Mother & Baby.

Adam King
Editor

Contents

Elizabeth Rachel Chuck	Learning To Crawl	1
S. Rees	Untitled	2
Karen Linskey	Becoming A Mum	3
A. Lydon	"Kaya"	4
J. Roberts	Letting Go	5
Wendy Webb	Terrible Two's And Threatening Three's	6
A. Clayton	For Ben	7
Joanne Eddie	Waiting	8
Elisabeth May Walley	Dinner All Around Me	9
Adele Claire Pugh	Guess Who?	10
Dianne Dixon	Motherhood	11
Rosemary Stewart	A Day In The Life Of A Childminder	12
Mark E. Hall	Kelly Jade Hall	13
Valerie Lloyd	Precious Gift	14
Paula Daines	Our Son Joe	15
Kelly Marie Horner	Rhianne	16
S. P. Cockayne	Acceptance	17
Emil Sebastian Ugarte	My Memoirs	18
W. Dabinett	Francesca's First	19
Margaret Cummings	Hannah Louise	20
Julie Clark	Untitled	21
Tracy Phillips	Fairies	22
Vera Jajechnyk	Bald, But Beautiful	23
Elijah, Hannah, Lisa & Michelle	Babies All Over	24
Dawn Porter	Milestones	25 / 26
B.Savory	Oh Goodness Me!	27
Belinda Mundy	Second Time Around	28 / 29
Jane Callaghan	Thoughts From An Older Mum	30
Susan Gadsby	Cope	31
J. Johnson	Last Drink Of The Day	32
Emma Wrigley	Untitled	33
Tina Muray	Don't Cry Over...	34
Glyn Traynor	Leah Jade Amber	35
Michael Yeardsley-Jones	A Very Special Gift	36 / 37
P. Mann	Baby Days	38
Fiona Locke	Flinn Rebecca Locke	39

Julie Smith	Untitled	40
Jacqueline Hartles	Daniel	41
J. A. Wiseman	Stephanie	42 / 43
Beverley Troughton	"No!"	44
Belinda Hunt	The First Week At Home	45
Julie Martin	'Oh My Baby'	46
Isobel Thornton	The Joy Of A Baby	47
Sharon Samuel	Untitled	48
L. Booth	No Words	49 / 50
Andrew Cundell	'D' Day	51
M. C. Darwin	Emily, Just Look At Her Now	52
Ruth Farber-Nathan	Featal Fart	53
Sara Fortey	I Have A Son	54
Joyce Sandell	Our Sunbeams	55
S. Holland	David	56
Julie Richardson	Wrapped With Love	57
Deborah Davis	Small Wonders	58
Pauline Ward	Our Little Angel	59
S. J. Sargent	The Months Of Discomfort Are Over	60 / 61
W. B. Burton	H.M.S.	62
Jenny Wehrle	Joshua	63
P. Duff	A Simple Question	64 / 65
Beverley Stephenson	Our Son Thomas Bradley Stephenson	66
Leanne Toone	Born To Soon	67
Jayne Atkinson	Our Baby	68
Noreen Burke	Spring Suprise	69
Valerie Downs	Paul	70
Kim Perring	My Son	71
Lewis	Cora Nancy	72
Nicky Jane Blundell	Where Do Babies Come From?	73
S. Douglas	Wonderment	74
Alison Ford	Katie	75
Nicola Jarvis	Flooding Feelings	76
Samantha Griffiths	Pain And Pleasure	77
E. J. Morrison	Jessica	78
Jackie Mann	Babe	79
Wilburt Wagtail	Poor Billy	80 / 81
Terry Blythe	Absurd	82
V. Rucastle	Untitled	83

D. C. S.	Grandma And R. J.	84 / 85
V. J. McTigue	Parenthood	86
J. L. Smit	A Mothers Love	87
Beverley Elliot	Birth Day	88
Rosemary Wood	Bedtime	89
Linda Santini	Child Of My Life	90
V. Thompson	Roxanne	91
D. Hickinbottom	Christopher Says	92
E. V. Benning	Untitled	93
Catherine Bigland	Baby Blues	94
J. Chadwick	Twins	95
Lindsay Allen	The Awakening	96
Jayne Sears	Ours And Baby's View	97
Helen Stuart	Untitled	98
Cindy C. Devlin	Stephenie	99
J. M. Macsween	The Precious Year	100
A. E. Bolton	For Serené	101 / 102
Paula Ryder	Ode To Katie	103
Jeremy D. Michaels	Will You Be	104

Learning To Crawl

Oh yes indeed I've learned to crawl
Now I can drive them up the wall.
I can get into cupboards and onto the stairs
Put toast in my toy box, be sick under chairs.
You might hear the cat give a mighty big wail
As I give a violent tug on his tail.
If there's money about, with it I'll play
There's nothing I'd rather be doing today.
I've stolen a hairbrush, a shoe and a paper
Oh yes I'm really enjoying this caper.
What on earth is this dish, oh goody it's cake
If I put it in the video do you think it'll bake?
I can get in the kitchen and steal pots and pans
I can get in the bin and dirty my hands.
I've just covered the floor in cotton wool
Eaten a gas bill, goodness I'm full.
I've discovered that baby wipes taste very nice
Much better than smelly old baby rice.
What's on this plate? Oh yummy pet food
If I eat it all will the cat think I'm rude?
How many fingers will fit in this socket?
Will daddy be cross if I empty his pocket?
they think their life is hard but I've only just begun
Soon I'll be walking, lucky me, what fun!

Elizabeth Rachel Chuck

Untitled

A long time ago when I was small
My Mum wrote this poem to me.
She wanted for me something to keep
from her especially.
She says that I was beautiful
She says that I was the best
She'll always think I'm beautiful
And lovelier than the rest
She wanted to say how special I was
and that she'll always care.
She wanted to say how special I was
and always she'd be there.
She also wanted to be sure,
that I'd always know,
She didn't love me on her own -
My Daddy loves me so.
So when I grow up and try to be me,
I'm to read this to be sure,
that whoever I turn out to be,
they'll love me even more.
And when I'm feeling lonely,
or ever far from home,
I'm to read this to remember,
I'm never on my own.

S Rees

Becoming A Mum

My feelings overwhelm me,
all I could do was cry,
after nine months of waiting he was mine!
No longer just an auntie, I didn't have to give him back,
So for the first night I lay awake to look at my beautiful little chap.

As morning came, I was still excited, his father delighted.
Feeling tired I tried to rest, but baby had other ideas,
he knew best.

Now three years have gone, and we have another son.
I still shed a tear when I think back to the day,
I became a mum

Karen Linskey

"Kaya"

From a little fluttering butterfly,
To an Eric Cantona,
I felt you kick and grow inside me,
Giggling at your hiccups,
And wondering what you'd look like.
I went to Mcdonald's on Sunday,
Then had you early Monday.
I actually enjoyed the labour,
It felt wonderful.
You're six months old now,
It still feels wonderful.

A Lydon

Letting Go

This morning I handed you over
      To someone new.
I came back home
      What shall I do?
You held my hand
      Grown up and smart.
I love you, little boy
      With all my heart.
Your toys lie scattered
      Around the room.
It seems so quiet
      So full of gloom.
I look at the clock
      I feel such a fool.
It's time to collect you
      From your first day at school.

J. Roberts

Terrible Two's And Threatening Three's

Bouncing the bed, with dawn breaking,
Squealing "Day", he turns on the light;
Insists you know it's "Next morning",
As you groan and beg him, "Night, night".

He knows so well Potty Training
And will tell you, grinning, "Wee, wee";
Drops soggy pants on the table,
After he has finished his pee.

But, woe betide, when it's "Poo, poo",
For there is no warning at all;
Except a silence and straining
And burnt dinner smells in the hall.

He rushes the weekly shopping,
Loading tins and bottles with glee;
Keenly he fills up the trolley
With "milkshake" roast dinner and tea.

Bedtime is just a disaster
Of flannels and suds on the floor;
Sodden hair foaming with toothpaste,
As you skid on soap through the door.

But then you Dose Up with "Bonding"
And vow that it's really worthwhile;
Your cherub is sleeping soundly,
Dreaming of his next mucky pile.

Wendy Webb

For Ben

His big brown eyes look lovingly,
so innocent and small.
For his little tantrums,
so easily I fall.
Just to love and cherish him,
sets my heart aglow.
So, much pleasure, I will get,
as I watch him grow.
In his life he'll have so much love
but, his love will outshine.
As he grows he will realise,
I am so proud he's mine.

A. Clayton

Waiting

We're having a baby
We are now three
We're having a baby
What will it be?

The family standing by
Love and care in their hearts
Myself and my husband
Wetting our pants!

We hope that we'll make it
The three of us until then
And nothing goes wrong
That the doctors can't mend.

It's highly amazing
This child growing inside
The love from the two of us
We just cannot hide.

We're having a baby
We just cannot wait
We're having a baby
Christmas is the date!

Joanne Eddie

Dinner All Around Me

There's dinner on my fingers and dinner on my toes,
And dinner all around me and even up my nose,
You gave my dinner to me and I give it back to you,
I need my dinners inside me to help me make the day through (oh yes I
do).
I love my dinners I really do,
They make me windy and they make me poo.
There's booby bottled and munchies too,
And all that food for me to chew.

Elisabeth May Walley

9

Guess Who?

Five little fingers, five little toes
A fat little face and a cute button nose
Plump little cheeks, twinkling eyes of blue
One little person - all shiny and new!

Laughs and chuckles, gurgles and coos
Precious memories that we'll never lose.
Golden curls, a gorgeous smile
Little Princes Charming, born to beguile.

Four months old and as good as gold,
A cheeky little fella, he's broken the mould!
Hugs and cuddles and perhaps a kiss,
Spending time together is absolute bliss.

Who am I talking about? Should I confess?
Do you know who I mean? Can you guess... ?
He's our new baby, our pride and joy
He's little Joseph - our beautiful baby boy!

Adele Claire Pugh

MotherHood

When I first found out,
I went into shock,
But I started to knit,
A shawl and a sock.

As time went by,
I got bigger and bigger,
Oh, what has happened,
To my once slim figure.

The big day was here,
And I finally gave birth,
But, oh, how I feel like
I pushed heaven and earth.

I look down in my arms,
At my bundle of joy,
My very own baby,
A beautiful boy.

Now it's time to go home,
And I shed a small tear,
But the nurse cheers me up,
She says 'See you next year!'.

Dianne Dixon

A Day In The Life Of A Childminder

Today, I sat, I ate my lunch, with not one of my usual bunch
Emma in bed, Janet asleep, Rachel at Playschool, not a peep.
My sandwich, my crisps, my apple I ate, listening for the sound of the
back gate.
Elaine, Andrew and Rachel draw near, lunch will be hectic, as usual, I
fear.
A roll, a yoghurt an apple, for two, and for Emma..
Soup and yoghurt will do.
Nappies, Sesame Street and then half past three
Thomas is home, we all watch T.V.
Five o'clock seems so far away, at last they've all gone.. no more for
today.
Tea I will cook, fish, turkey or ham, or maybe a sandwich with honey or
jam.
Thursday is over, Friday draws near, soon it's the weekend....
LET'S HEAR A BIG CHEER!!!!!!!!!!

Rosemary Stewart

Kelly Jade Hall

Kisses and cuddles,
Especially for you,
Little, sweet and
Lovable,
Your so beautiful too !

Just a few days old,
And so small and new,
Daughter, Grandchild, Niece,
Everyone loves you !

Happiness you've brought us,
And we love you more each day,
Little 'Kelly Jade Hall',
Love you, what else can we say ?

Mark E. Hall

Precious Gift

Oh baby, baby small and sweet
You have made my life complete.
Just a bundle in a shawl
Lying there so pink and small.
You have made me realise
How great is God, how good, how wise.
What a miracle you are
The best thing ever made by far.
So perfect in every way
My only prayer is that I may
Be given guidance, that I might
Always know how to treat you right.
It's easy now while your so small
You're not a problem now at all.
But what about as you grow older
The things you do get bigger, bolder.
Will I then be shown the way
The right and proper things to say.
To guide you to a perfect life
To guard you from too much strife.
Show you how to love your maker
Be a giver not a taker.
We have so much too face
I only pray we stand the pace.
To come out on the other side
With no conscience we must hide.

Valerie Lloyd

Our Son Joe

Labour started just before two
At last, the baby was already overdue
The pains were getting regular
Every five minutes or so
Better get to the hospital
Not long to go.
Arrived at the hospital around eight that morning
Just as other new babies were waking and yawning
Admitted and prepared, then put to bed
"Now to the delivery room" a young midwife said.
The day was going fast and night was drawing near
"I can see the babies head" my husband said with a cheer.
In that same labour ward just before eight
A little boy was born, he just couldn't wait.
He'd waited and waited for most of the day
And decided it was time to come out and play.
A son for us both, what a joy
We'd always hoped for a little boy.
Eight pounds he weighed, what a size
We both cuddled our son with tears in our eyes.
My mum and dad were the first to know
They had a healthy grandson who was going to be called 'Joe'.

Paula Daines

Rhianne

When she was born not so long ago
I knew that she would be, the bearer of such happiness
to her new found family.

Although she does not realise, or know what she has done,
She's helped with a small miracle, the rising of the sun.

God gave us an angel, to help us ease the pain
He's given us the gift of love, sunshine where there was rain.

Not many people understand the love that she has given,
But you would love an angel, if God sent you one from heaven.

Her eye's are like the clearest sea, yet they sparkle like the stars,
Her hair sprinkled with angel dust, the most beautiful by far.

When she smiles your heart just soars with love
Any pain you felt is gone
We'd like to thank the moon and stars, we've got our little one.

I hope one day she reads this ode
In honour of her name
And no matter what the future holds, we'll love her just the same.

Whenever she is lonely, if she ever needs a friend
She's got a mum and dad that love her
And on whom she can depend.

Kelly Marie Horner

Acceptance

It's a girl the midwife cried,
My husband held my hand and sighed.
She's lovely, well done he said,
And I thanked God, and lay back on the bed.
This tiny bundle that now was born
Had first seen light at the hour of dawn.
Is she all-right was the next thing I said
The eyes that looked down seemed full of dread.
The words they now uttered were filled with pain.
I'm so sorry dear, but there is something wrong.
I am afraid she's brain damaged.
I bit hard on my tongue.
My head was a whirl, I felt dizzy and sick.
The clock on the wall seemed to give a loud tick.
The silence around screamed louder than words.
I looked out of the window and watched the birds.
Our baby our precious our bundle of joy.
She was brain damaged just like our boy.
But I knew with every nerve in my body
That our little girl would be somebody.
She would be, our pride and joy,
Just the same as our little boy.

S. P. Cockayne

My Memoirs

I was made out of love by my daddy and mummy
- For almost nine months I grew inside her tummy
Then one day, in theatre, a man with a knife
Cut me out of my "swimming pool" granted me life
- It's seventeen weeks since the day I came home
And you wouldn't believe just how much I have grown!
When my dad's got a migraine I yell and I shout
Giving screams of frustration when mummy goes out
If I know they're exhausted, it's my time to play
- Oh, I bet there's been times they could give me away....
I fill all my nappies the moment they're on
Or wee over grandma - that <u>really</u> is fun!
My eyes are the shape of my big brothers, TIm
I've my daddy's "basque" nose and my mummy's small chin
My fingers are granddad's, all slender and fine
- So which parts of me have I got that are mine?
When I'm all nice and cosy, it's time for my bath
So how come they want me to lie there and laugh?
But I win them both round with my big, toothless grin
As I try to make sense of this world that I'm in
- I'm surrounded by love and by people who care
And so glad to be part of this family I share....

Emil Sebastian Ugarte (Aged 17½ Weeks)

Francesca's First

This year has passed so quickly for Mum and Dad
It seems like only yesterday a babe in arms we had.

You have put new meaning to our lives made it richer it is true
Each day is a pleasure to share it with you.

It has been a joy this year watching you grow
Into the little girl we love and have come to know.

Your first smile, your words and the steps you take
Are nothing compared to the laughter you make.

You win peoples heart's, the star of any place
Always happy and jolly with a smile upon your face.

The compliments you receive puts us on the ninth cloud
To be your parents makes us feel so proud.

So we treasure each day and behold the memory
As we look forward to know what the future will be.

W. Dabinett

Hannah Louise

She stares at me and wonders why
With these tears I try and hide.
If she only knew the truth
Just what happened in her youth.
How cold and empty inside I feel
But as time goes on I know I'll heal.
My love for her grows stronger each day
When I give my time and we sit and play.
The sound of her chuckles and her laughter too
Makes me feel warm again and I feel new.
A smile will come across my face
No-one in the world can take her place.
She'll stay deep in this heart of mine
Until the very end of time.

Margaret Cummings

Untitled

They can hear you stir up a cup of tea,
They can hear you butter bread,
They can even hear you close your eyes
Or rest your weary head.
Their ears tune in to all these sounds,
They begin to stir and wake.
You see all these tell-tale noises,
Mean that mummy is taking a break!

Julie Clark

Fairies

Last night some fairies came into your bedroom,
They waved their wands and cast a magic spell.
Then whispered in your ear some words of wisdom.
And made you promise that you wouldn't tell.
At least that's how I'd like to think it happens.
When babies give their mummy a surprise.
By showing us that childhood's not forever.
And growing up before our very eyes.

Tracy Phillips

Bald, But Beautiful

Sam's gummy smile
his toothless grin,
can melt your heart
it's a beautiful thing.

That little bald head
with practically no hair,
is so appealing,
Sam's very fair.

Sam's toothless, but cute.
Bald, but beautiful.
With an inner glow.
I love him so!

Vera Jajechnyk

Babies All Over

Babies babies the world is full of babies,
Babies play,
baies eat,
babies drink and go to sleep.
Babies are cute,
babies are small,
babies are loved by one and all.

Babies suck their little thumbs,
babies often cry for their mums.
Babies like a little nap,
babies like to terrorise the cat.
Babies wear pampers nappies,
and when they grow up,
they get very happy.

Elijah, Hannah, Lisa & Michelle (Aged 8 / 9)

Milestones

One minute a baby, the next a little boy,
From lying there just looking to holding a toy
The changes are amazing, they happen so fast,
Each new thing he learns is certainly not the last!

He's now two months old, and is happy all the while
It's rare that he cries, and he's always got a smile
He goes out in his pram, wrapped up against the cold
People say 'Time fly's', make the most of him I'm told.

He's now four months old, and loves splashing in the bath
And gets excited, when his dad walks down the path
Weaning him has started, he really likes the taste
He likes his food so much, there's rarely any waste.

He's now six months old and he sits up on his own
We really can't believe how quickly he has grown
He used to feed on my knee, now sits in a chair
He's also started crawling and now gets everywhere.

He's now eight months old and his teeth are coming through
Yesterday there was just one, and now there are two
He used all the furniture to help him to stand
Getting down is easy, his bottom helps him land.

He's now ten months old and he's such a cheeky lad
Whenever he's around, I can never feel sad
When I say 'No don't do that', he gives a grin
And goes and does it anyway, empties the bin!

He's nearly one, our little boy - one year old
We do make the most of him, just like we were told
He's changed and grown so fast, learning from mum and dad
We wouldn't be without him, our precious little lad.

Dawn Porter

Oh Goodness Me!

I must learn this, I must learn that,
I can't do this, I can't do that,
If I say this, will I get that?
Oh goodness me!

Give a smile here, give a smile there,
Just walk here, just walk there,
If I play here, can I go there?
Oh goodness me!

Eat a bit more, eat a bit less,
Sleep a bit more, sleep a bit less,
If I laugh more, do I cry less?
Oh goodness me!

Give mummy a kiss, give daddy a cuddle,
Give me a kiss, I want a cuddle,
All these rules a baby must learn,
Oh goodness me!

B. Savory

Second Time Around

I knew about the sleepless nights
I knew about the crying
I did it all the first time round
I thought it would be fine.

But here I am now, wide awake
3 o'clock in the morning
Why does it feel such a shock,
As if I had no warning?

'Try to rest when he's asleep'
That's what they always say
What do I tell my little girl
Who wants 'Mummy to play'.

She loves her little brother
He's here now and that's fine
But why does mummy seem to be
With him all the time?

Of course, it does get better
A whole nights sleep in bed
The world always looks brighter
With a clearer head.

And then, one day it happens
He gives you that first smile
Reward for all that effort
It starts to feel worthwhile.

So now, I've got two children
It's harder than it sounds
But the great moments are just as great
The Second Time Around

Belinda Mundy

Thoughts From An Older Mum

Motherhood for the second time round at forty-two,
But this time I'm not alone - I have a husband and daughter too.
We reject all the tests, as an abortion would not be considered,
But we offer up constant prayers until our baby is safely delivered.
An elective section - it's a boy,
We both shed tears of joy.
Matthew's perfect and a source of delight,
Even though he stays awake all night.
So older mums who leave it later,
It's exhausting but your experience is greater.
From the moment they cut the cord
A beautiful baby is your reward.

Jane Callaghan

Cope

An aggrophobic for nine years
Never venturing out
Feeling unwell, sick and tired,
Phoning a friend "Any bug about"
Weeks later to no away
I'm pregnant with no.5 on the way
How will I cope
How will I plan
How will I get on having a scan
Nothing to worry, everything's fine
I gave birth to Jordan at 20 past 9
Infact it's done me good
I didn't think it would
All the scars of going out
Makes me realize what life is all about.

Susan Gadsby

Last Drink Of The Day

Babies are cute, babies are sweet
But somehow they just don't, stay very neat.
they're sick on their clothes and dribble all day
Sometimes I wish, they knew what they wanted to say
They're day starts with breakfast
O' dear what a task
Food on their faces that looks like a mask
Then soon it's sleep time, sometimes we hope
A few jobs done - how will I cope?
Only done the washing then their awake
My God! It's lunchtime, no time to bake.
Next comes their tea, much better this time
But they're only pretending, what a good mime
For next is the time of the day for a cry
Two hours long - take a big sigh
Not long till bath time - o' what a joy
Get soaking wet and hit by a toy
The last drink of the day, lots of warm milk
Their eyes are all heavy, their skin feels like silk.
Then they drift off to sleep, time to sit down and rest
The time of day I like the best
A nice hot bath, a cup of tea
Then off to bed and sleep for me
The next day brings a cry nice and early
Then a great big smile, their teeth all purly
Now I know, why we women give birth
To have all the love and a life full of mirth.

J. Johnson

Untitled

You... have no memory of your own importance
Not now, not then
When
Out of my body you came falling with
Yesterday's necessities.
And when you yawn, your breath is
Nothing if not empty and simple
... but all complexity
And I love you.

Emma Wrigley

Don't Cry Over...

Tears stream down my face,
As wasted milk from swollen breast's
Washes over flattened stomach,
Across a scar that brought you here.
Empty belly
Empty heart
I shower, sing my song to you,
Louder now - as not womb-encased
But further away.

Tina Murray

Leah Jade Amber

You were born
And they took you away
Tiny lungs did not fill, nor chest rise
Then   LIFE!
You battled on, and made us proud.
Vivid flower of happiness
Showering sparkling stars of love upon us
You are beautiful
And I can see both of ours in your tiny face
We feel the loss of you, little girl
But Daddy says you're a gorgeous flower -
We will always have the flower
Though your scent dances in a further field.

Glyn Traynor

A Very Special Gift

We'd been trying for years without a glimmer of hope,
Thinking, if we never had children could we really cope?

The very thought would make us dejected and sad,
A part of our lives that we never had.

Every month would go by we would pray for the time,
That the pregnancy test would show a blue line.

I remember that day when I felt so proud,
Next door even heard me I shouted that loud.

An appointment is made for the very first scan,
A tear in the eye of a very proud man.

It all seems so strange after such a long wait,
A picture to see, confirmation and date.

We both can't believe it, it just seems all a blare,
We're pregnant "A baby" a new life to share.

Scans, tests, checking everything's fine,
Little fingers and toes inspiring this rhyme.

Lets decorate the Nursery paint the walls and the ceiling,
We just can't explain what it is we are feeling.

Pastel colours, clowns and balloons on a string,
A few toys for baby, nursery rhymes to sing.

Cotton buds, wet wipes, vaseline and oil,
Special sized nappies for baby to soil.

Babygrows, bibs, mittens and dummy,
Breast feeding tips, sore nipples for mummy.

Parentcraft classes and advice for that day,
Panting and pushing, we'll just have to pray.

Pregnancy suits her I think she looks swell,
It's only her lump, that's how you can tell.

Something we've wanted since we've been together.
Our very own baby we'll cherish forever.

Michael Yeardsley-Jones

Baby Days

One of the best things that can happen in life
Is to find a true love and make her your wife
Then one day a little body comes along
Hits your household like a bomb.
Your usual tranquil life has gone
Now its all nappies, bottles, and rusks
Takes mum and dad a while to adjust
He gets the gripes, cry's at night, and can be sick
To order. This is what babies do, to try the
Patience of their mother and their father
Then one day you'll see him smile
And know that its all worthwhile.
Try to enjoy every stage
These are memories for your old age
Remember every funny face he pulls
Remember every burp.
Remember when he cuts his first tooth
And when he starts to walk
Then the best day you've ever had
He'll smile at you and for the first time
He'll say dad.
So enjoy your little offspring
Enjoy his babydays while you can.
Because before you know it
He'll have grown into a man
When he looks back on the childhood he had
He'll remember how much he was loved by
His mum and his dad.

P. Mann

Flinn Rebecca Locke -Born 3.11.95

The night they told us you had died
Words just cannot say;
We cried the river of your life
But still you'd gone away.
The hours of pain to bring you out
Just to give you up;
Couldn't hold your beauty when we met
For fear we'd never let you go -
Now I cry the ocean of your life
With a love that sears my soul.
Our arms, my breasts, they long for you
An ache no-one can fill,
But wherever you've gone
You'll always be
Our beloved, first born, baby girl.

x o x

Fiona Locke

Untitled

Sick
Dizzy
Tired
Irritable
Test
Blue
Shock !

Clinic
Tests
Heartburn
Rest
Fat
Waddling
Bored !

Waiting
Endless
Midwife
Pain
Excitement
Relief
Baby !

Eyes
Blue
Beautiful
Smiling
Mouth
Gurgling
Crying
Kicking
Restless
Chubby
Arms
Waving
Happy
Content
Perfect
Sleeping
Baby
Son.

Julie Smith

Daniel

Our little precious,
    Our little boy,
        Our little Daniel,
            No little love.

Mummy's little angel,
    Daddy's little man,
        Perfect little gift,
            Beautiful little son.

Such a lot of love,
    For one little child,
        Our little lad,
            Our little Dan.

Jacqueline Hartles

Stephanie

Our darling daughter, you are one today,
We love you much more than words can say,
You are a miracle to us, sent from above,
A joy to us both, a true gift of love.

The day you were born, we cuddled you tight,
Knowing at once, we loved you at first sight,
You were small and helpless but so divine,
A daughter, a friend, our ray of sunshine.

To see you learn and to watch as you've grown,
You have touched our hearts in a way never known,
You have given us love, joy and happiness too,
How could we have known how much we'd love you?

You're full of smiles and such a treasure,
A bundle of fun, who gives everyone pleasure,
From your smile and your touch to your gentle kiss,
We never thought we could be as happy as this.

You had a great grandma, so proud she'd have been,
To see you named after her - Stephanie Kathleen,
She'll be there to protect you and watch over you too,
Every day and every night in all that you do.

A place in her heart there will always be,
For the great-granddaughter she was never to see
We want you to know that we will always be here,
To love and support you in each coming year.

A wonderful year and so many good times we have had,
Happy Birthday sweetheart, with love, Mum and Dad.

J. A. Wiseman

"No!"

No! is the usual word I hear myself say
to a little terror who never gets his own way.
With back to the floor and legs in the air,
I cry "Help", give me strength and phone agony aunt Claire.

Beverley Troughton

The First Week At Home

Returning to bed after the umpteenth feed
I hear my baby cry.
Or do I?

Everyday noises distort in my head
To sound like my baby's cry:
The whine of a jet as it starts to descend;
The washing machine winding up for a spin;
The yap of a dog patrolling his street;
The call of a bird on the telephone wire;
The scream of a toddler expressing frustration;
And a motorbike roaring ahead of the queues.

I must learn to relax.
Switch off.
Unwind.
And rest while my baby's asleep.
Because once she starts, there's no mistaking
The sound of my baby's cry.

Belinda Hunt

'Oh My Baby'

The first words I said
When I came round
after the anaesthetic
Don't suppose it was an original line
Just seemed apt
Seemed to embrace every emotion I felt,
The love
The protection
The fulfilment
The emptiness of the womb
The start of a new life.

Julie Martin

The Joy Of A Baby

A tiny 'form' before your eyes,
Is what we first may see.
Tiny hands and tiny feet,
And quiet as can be.

A few weeks later down the line
Our little 'form' has grown
Moving, smiling, coo-ing now
The likes we've never known.

Rolling, crawling, peek-a-boo
And silly nursery rhymes
This all brings joy and laughter
And lots of happy times.

And just as quick as quick can be
This little person stands
And reaches out to walk with you
With those tiny hands.

Isobel Thornton

Untitled

Because he has a lovely grin
and dark brown eyes and olive skin
Because he brightens up my day
and loves a cuddle come what may.

He's only ten weeks old but already I can see
how much he's changed my life - and me
In the middle of the night when he wants to be fed
It's not even an effort to get out of bed.

I spend my time watching him - sometimes in tears
How did we manage without him over the years
My heart just melts at the thought of him
My beautiful baby - Benjamin.

Sharon Samuel

No Words

No words can describe my feelings for you.
The way that you are, the things that you do.
Perfect, beautiful, incredible; they all seem to fit.
They're all very apt, but not quite it.
Proud and privileged, the way you make me feel.
These words say it all, but have no appeal.

No words can describe our new life together.
Fantastic and wonderful, now and forever.
But still this isn't quite what I want to say.
Life's simply brilliant, day after day.
And yet my feelings cannot be written.
For since that first day, I've been totally smitten.

No words can describe the love in my heart.
My life seems so empty when we're apart.
Magnificent and magical, the moment I see you again.
But these words won't do and I've racked my brain.
Unbelievable and astounding, your baby face.
Your warm personality lights up this place.

No words can describe the day of your birth.
There can be nothing as miraculous on God's earth.
I watch as you develop and grow.
What do you think? What do you know?
The noises you make, what are you trying to say?
What words would you use if you had your way?

No words can describe, my heart full of pride.
That wonderful glow when you're by my side.
You're my pride and joy, my love, my son.
You bring me such happiness, such pleasure, such fun.
I could search and search my whole life through.
But the words that fit the best are "I Love You".

L. Booth

'D' Day

The day is in your diary,
It's on the calendar on the wall,
You've told all your friends and family,
I've paid the phone bill for them all!

Now 'D' days getting closer,
The hours tick away,
Cross days off on the calendar,
It's closer day by day.

And when it's time for 'D' day,
The excitement will be high,
Just look down at your tummy,
'Cos the pain's going to make you cry!

And when the day is over,
They'll be new life on this Earth,
The champagne will be flowing,
For the miracle of birth.

BUT that's only if your lucky,
Because no-one will really know,
What time baby decides to move,
And come out to say 'Hello'.

Andrew Cundell

Emily, Just Look At Her Now

Just look at her now,
Sat upright - no slouching there!
With a toy in her hand, her
Hand in her hair.

She turns and crawls
The sofa her aim,
With a pull from her hands
She's up again.
Then down she drops to retrieve her toy,
And up again
Just look at her now.

She takes my hands
A grin on her face
And off she goes at her own steady pace
My seven month baby is trying to walk
So much to learn in such a short space
Of time, just look at her now.

M. C. Darwin

Featal Fart

Today I found out something quite funny,
that baby's when they are in the tummy,
not only kick and grow but drink,
now this small fact has made me think,
and now I've kind'a made a link,
if baby drinks, must pee and poo,
and the mystery's solved for me and you,
I've finally done it I've made the link
it's the baby <u>not me</u> who's making that stink!

Ruth Farber-Nathan

I Have A Son

I have a son.

I'm tired but I can't sleep,
I'm happy but I want to weep.

Beside me lies the cause of my emotional mix,
a tiny bundle a few hours old.
I wonder, can I have a hold?
Is it permitted?
What will the midwife say?
As a "new" mum, I'm not sure what I'm allowed to do today.

Today, is Thomas' birth day.
I am a Mum.
My life will never be the same.
Oh dear, what if he doesn't like his name?

I've got responsibilities,
I've got a son.
Oh dear, what have I done?

I never expected to feel like this,
The bond I feel for him is so strong.
Not surprising as I've waited to see him for so long,
but worries and doubts are also there.
What kind of mother will I be?

I guess we'll have to wait and see.

I have a son.

Sara Fortey

Our Sunbeams

Two little rays of sunshine
came into our lives this year.
You should have seen them lying there
it made me shed a tear.

One little ray went dimmer
and all our prayers were there,
to help her gather all her strength
and let her know we care.

Those nurses need a medal.
Their patience love and care,
they helped that tiny heart to beat
while she was staying there.

One very long month later,
Lois came back home at last.
Now she's with her sister Lucy
and growing really fast.

I'm not a holy person
but way back then in March.
I wondered if there was a God
and needed his help fast.

All I can say is 'thankyou'
for no one knows what it means.
To see those rays of sunshine now
who smile like big sunbeams.

Joyce Sandell

David

The soft brown hair
The sorrowful stare.

The baby blue eyes
The midnight cry's.

The tiny fingers and toes
The snotty nose.

The playful laugh
The tearful bath.

The sweet dreams
The teething screams.

All the reason why
You're the apple of my eye.

S. Holland

Wrapped With Love

When you was born you let out a yawn
As though you was bored or maybe even ignored:

But all I could do was to weep
As I held on to your tiny feet:

Then I whispered you are so sweet
You looked so soft as you went of to sleep:

Your hair was thin and fair:
Your eyes were brown and perfectly round:

As your tears fell down and then around
Your soft pale checks:
As you lay there with a frown:

Now I send a special gift
To my one and only you:
A box of kisses wrapped with love
For the one I love that you.

Julie Richardson

Small Wonders

When you gaze into your babies eyes,
You know you have won first prize.
The wonder of it all.
From someone very small.

What a delight it is to be,
When they stand up with glee.
Those first wobbly steps,
Gives joy to your hearts deepest depths.

Deborah Davis

Our Little Angel

Life will never be the same,
Everything was calm before he came.

He gives us love, he gives us joy,
Ryan John, our baby boy.

He's into everything he sees,
Climbing, walking or on his knees.

You know what he wants, though he can't say a word,
He manages to get his wishes heard.

Such a happy smile and bright blue eyes,
He's even gorgeous when he cries.

He loves to play with all his toys,
And Boy oh Boy, what a noise.

When the day is over and its time for bed,
Ryan lays down his sweet weary head.

Within a few minutes you can hear him snore,
Then that's it until morning, peace once more.

Dedicated to Ryan John Ward Born 11.10.95

Pauline Ward

The Months Of Discomfort Are Over

The months of discomfort are over
The sickness and the back pain
My body has totally changed
Life will never be the same again.

The doubts about my capability
The total change of my life
Its a very big step
To become a Mother as well as a wife.

To be responsible for a child
To have to teach them right from wrong
Its the most important job of all
And I know I need to be strong.

If love was all that was needed
Then I know things would be fine
I've never known a love like it
I just can't believe that your mine.

My heart is overflowing
With the love I feel for you
But I worry about your future
And the things that I might not do.

There are so many things to teach you
So much that you'll need to know
To mould you into a good person
So much you need to be shown.

I can only do my best for you
To let you feel loved, safe and secure
If love is all it takes
You'll turn out fine, I'm sure.

S. J. Sargent

H.M.S.

At first a wee bump in your tum
Nine months later you became a Mum
To your surprise a little girl
But not as yet with the deadly curl
I wonder how she'll speak and sound
I wonder how she'll run around
I'll bet she'll be a little snob
Much better than a flamin' yob
We know at least she's very pretty
And her nappies haven't been that gritty
But only 'cos she's like her Mum
Well she would be - coming from her tum.

W. B. Burton

Joshua

When we first saw our baby boy
      Our hearts were filled with love and joy.
A unique child, perfect and sweet
      He made our family so complete.

His tiny cries would break my heart
      But this, it seems, was just the start,
He loved the food which came from me,
      This brought us closer naturally.

The special bond between us grew,
      I'd gaze at him with love anew.
Our little boy was growing fast -
      I willed the newborn-stage to last.

But, he was changing everyday
      Starting to gurgle and to play;
Recognition in that first smile
      Made every wakeful night worthwhile.

Now he laughs, blows a big bubble,
      Plays with toys, gets into trouble!
From newborn baby, small and curled
      He's still the best in the whole wide world.

Jenny Wehrle

A Simple Question

I'd like to ask a question, mam
I really must find out
Tell me where I come from, mam
So I'll know without a doubt.

That's a very grown up question, son
To ask how you began
I'll do my best to tell you, son
And explain as best as I can.

You were not brought by gypsies, son
In the middle of the night
You did not appear by magic, son
Or in a blinding flash of light.

The stork did not carry you, son
In beak, from clouds to me
You did not arrive by post, son
That's not the way you see.

The story is quite simple, son
Your Mammy and your Da'
Created life from love, son
From all the joys there are.

A baby we had made, son
And it grew inside of me
A little boy was born, son
That's how you came to be.

What are you on about, our mam
You can make up such tales
Now tell me where I come from, mam
Bill said he's from Wales!

P. Duff

Our Son Thomas Bradley Stephenson

Our Angels delight,
Our child so bright,
Stole our hearts at a quarter to midnight.

Once he was there, a boy so fair,
(Thomas Bradley Stephenson)
All we could do was stare.

His tiny hands, his golden hair,
Our prayers had finally been answered.

Now our child so tall so handsome
Our parents so proud to call him their Grandson.

A smile so bright,
A cuddle so tight,
"I love you Mammy, Daddy, God Bless and Good Night".

"Good Morning" he says first thing with a smile,
"Is it OK if we play for a while".

We look at each other my husband and I,
Aren't we so lucky we gave it another try....

Beverley Stephenson

Born To Soon

The labour has started, you know it's too soon
For baby to leave his mother's womb

My baby is born, so tiny and frail
His skin so translucent and horribly pale

A tube in his mouth to help him breath
You can't yet bring yourself to believe

It's hard to believe when racked with emotion
But constant the care from staff with devotion

A rollercoster ride is the only way
To describe how you cope from day to day

And then from somewhere there comes some hope
His monitor's gone, he's starting to cope

At last he's come home it's out time to care
Those magical moments for us to share

He's 22 months old now, a cheeky little boy
We'll always be grateful for bringing us joy

Leanne Toone

Our Baby

Will you be a baby boy?
Or will you be a girl?
Will you have straight hair,
Or will you have some curls -
I've sorted through a pile of clothes,
The jumpers, trousers and the shirts
The vests, the socks, the hats 'n' things
Frilly dresses, and the skirts -
Will your eyes be green like Daddy's,
Or a shade of blue like mine?
Maybe, even brown ones, well,
We shall see in time.
Will you be a crier
Or be as good as gold,
Will you do just as you please,
Or do as you are told.
Will you learn to crawl around
Before you learn to walk.
What will your little voice sound like,
When you can "Baby-talk"!
But, whatever you are like my child,
You're special; our first one,
And we'll love our
Darling Daughter, or
Our Precious Little Son... *xxx*

Jayne Atkinson

Spring Suprise

Too early! She arrived. One spring day.
Bursting into the world, our Lorna Mae.
With eyes of blue, and hair so fair.
She changed our lives. Our little prayer.

With nappies, bottles, Barney on TV.
My days are different. No time for me.
But oh! Such happiness, such joy is now ours.
Because of a little girl. Who arrived with the flowers.

Noreen Burke

Paul

My beautiful baby with hair of gold
Although you are only nine months old,
You've brought to me much joy to treasure
Tears and laughter in equal measure.

Your laughter I've loved, your tears I've dried
And sometimes so full of love for you myself I've cried.
Your chubby hands and your smiling eyes
I'll remember forever as the years pass by.

You've brought to me such happiness
It's hard for me in words to express
That though you're the third born out of our love,
You hold the place in my heart that you're worthy of.

Valerie Downs

My Son

My son is so special that each waking day
I'm filled with the fear he'll be taken away
Its something I think of yet try not to show
But I love him so deeply and its silly I know

His life is so precious and my heart seems to swell
When things that he does shows he loves me aswell
He can be so cheeky but he's so full of fun
And I am so proud that he's my special son.

Kim Perring

Cora Nancy

Hair like sun on golden sand
Eyes like clear blue water
Skin as soft as pure white silk
That's my darling daughter

Cora smiles and Cora laughs
It moves me deep inside
Make's my own smile seem
A thousand miles wide.

Now I am complete
No longer part but whole
One second with my baby
Touches deep inside my soul

For me my life is perfect
As dear as it can be
From now until forever
My precious Cora and me.

Lewis

Where Do Babies Come From ?

Under a gooseberry bush,
In a stork's beak
Some big babies
Would make that stork weak.
At the end of a rainbow
With a pot of gold,
Some people believe that,
Or so I'm told.
A gift from heaven
Filled with celestial cloud,
It's hard to believe
When they're screaming aloud.
Made from parents love and dreams,
That's the best explanation
To me it seems.

Nicky Jane Blundell

Wonderment

For all that you mean
For the love inside
For all of the memories
For the times we will cry
For watching you move
And feeling your touch
For wanting to tell you
We love this much

For being the first to see you
We know its worth the wait
For hoping you're on time
But maybe you'll be late
For wanting to hold you close
And just to hear you cry
Knowing we won't always understand
But that we will always try

For every word that is written
To make these lines you read
For the child that has been created
It is hard to believe
That something so amazing
Can happen every minute of each day
And the clock will keep on ticking
Until in my arms you lay

S. Douglas

Katie

On the 21st of August
Into this world there came
Our beautiful little daughter
Kathryn Erica is her name.

Born by caesarean section
Six weeks premature
Weighing only four pounds and two ounces
A tiny girl for sure.

Now she's fifteen weeks old
And what a character is she
She pulls funny faces, sticks out her tongue
And tries to stand when placed on your knee.

She cries when she's bored and she's hungry
Or when she's filled her nappy
But now at last she sleeps at night
Which makes both her parents real happy.

She loves it when she's mobile
The rocker, the pram or the car
It's no wonder that we get tired out
The miles she's covered so far.

She's got lots of family and friends
About as many as eighty
And is loved very much by them all
That's our darling daughter dear Katie.

Alison Ford

Flooding Feelings

Love is a strange thing!
It happens when you least expect it,
And doesn't when you expect it most.
I look at my child in the Hospital cot,
And wonder why I feel so numb.
A helpless child is watching me with knowing eyes,
But all I feel is shellshocked.
She cries, accusingly, demanding my love,
And then it happened, without a word
Or a sign. A trickle of first recognition,
A tightening of ties first started nine months ago.
A feeling so deep, so wonderful, comes
Flooding in with the realisation that
Nothing will ever come between you or hurt her.
And then the tears come and you give way
To all your hopes and nightmares.
Worrying that you can never keep her happy.
Finally, as you cradle her in your arms
And feed her from your body,
The calm, unmistakable feeling of pure,
Unselfish love for this wonderful creation sets in,
And you wonder at the range of emotions
You can feel in the space of ten long minutes.

Nicola Jarvis

Pain And Pleasure

I'd gone to bed quite peacefully, then been woken with a jump
The pain sudden and unbearable and originating from my 'lump'
With apprehension I wake your dad, his eyes are wide and bright
I wonder if he's excited too or if it's just pure fright
We hastily move towards the car, aware of the journey ahead
The road seems very uneven and every bump makes me see red
On arrival at the hospital we're shown to a side room
Buy now every step is agony and your arrival is beginning to loom
I gratefully accept the gas and air and clench my fists in pain
I wonder how much more I can take before I go insane
Hours later and in a drugged haze, I ask if your going to be long
Then suddenly I realise that the urge to push is strong
The midwife coaxes, but I don't hear and then begin to shout
And with an immense feeling of relief your head finally pops out
I'm exhausted and in shock, but I'm swept away with joy
As I look down at your perfect face and see a beautiful baby boy!

Samantha Griffiths

Jessica

Jessica, you dear sweet thing
how can you possibly hope to win
there are so many things you'll need to do
to fulfil your parents dreams for you.

You'll need to be clever, talented, witty
musical, creative, academic, pretty!
articulate.... but not to chatty
distinctive character.... but not too batty!

You'll need to be spontaneous and not too "straight"
but we want you to be disciplined to control your own fate
we want you to be strong and bold, full of zest for living
but we want you to be soft and meek full of love and giving.

you should be positive and trusting
don't always fear the worst
yet be cautious with your precious life
always speak to your parents first!

You need to know what's right and wrong
what deeds are good and bad
but don't be too idealistic
then fall short like mum and dad!

Please don't grow up scarred and stressed
struggling to achieve what we think is best
our dreams are worth nothing - however well meant
unless you grow up happy, healthy.... content.

Dear Jessie.... there's so much that we need to do
to make sure that all you dreams come true!

E. J. Morrison

Babe

He sleeps again once more
a stir and then a snore
He shifts his head a little
then rests it like before
So peaceful in his rest
its when I love him best
His little face it seems
is fresh and full of dreams.

As he stirs and wakes
new noises now he makes
His arms reach out for love
and hands come from above
A cuddle and a kiss
not many does he miss
He looks as if to say
come on mum lets play.

The toys lie on the ground
the love is all around
In colours and in games
and teddies with odd names
The smiles and the laughter
for ever ever after

**To you my son with love
from those hands above**

Jackie Mann

Poor Billy

Do animals go to Heaven mam,
I mean like, when they die,
The Vicar, said they've all got souls
and the Vicar wouldn't lie.

He said they're all Gods creatures,
and deserve a fitting end,
A burial, a mound, a solemn prayer,
to mourn a faithful friend.

And when they pass the Pearly Gates,
and gaze back down on earth,
do they see their tended grave stones,
and realize their worth.

So has every little mousie, mam
and every pesky fly
got a grave in someone's garden,
where their little bodies lie.

When Billy our old dog died mam,
did you both choose a site,
it was in the middle of winter,
and snowed every single night.

And would Billy look down from Heaven mam,
and witness his own fate,
as dad dragged an extra bin bag
towards the garden gate.

Do animals get to Heaven mam,
I mean like, when they die,
because Billy was the bestest dog,
and I know you wouldn't lie.....

Wilburt Wagtail

Absurd

We walked and walked and walked and walked
We talked and talked and talked and talked
Debated, consternated, chewed over and mused
Reached the point where we were confused
What right had we to contemplate
The pros and cons of our child's fate

Handicaps and downs and serious matters
If they came to pass it would leave us in tatters
What should be overwhelming love and total joy
Gave way to feelings of worry for our boy
But now he's two and oh so much fun
And has been since reaching the ripe age of one

Our fears and concerns it seems were unfounded
Our love for dear Aidan is totally unbounded
So now we've gone and done it again
With the benefit of experience and a little less pain
Now would you believe it we're trying for a third
Oh, what silly people, that's really absurd.

Terry Blythe

Untitled

Babies are lovely
Babies are cute
Babies are born
In their birthday suit.

Some have no hair
Some have a lot
And most go to sleep
In a crib or a cot.

They laugh or they cry
Depending on their mood
They're upset because
They usually want their food.

They're fed by a bottle
Or by a breast
Then winded and changed
Mum always knows best.

They're cuddly and warm
And oh such a treasure
They bring joy to their parents
By filling them with pleasure.

This poem is written
To let you all know
That having babies is fun
So, come on, have a go!

V. Rucastle

Grandma And R.J.

Grandma immersed in book, foot idly,
Gently, rocking small chair
Holding sleeping grandson, four months
Old. First born of own dear girl --
Lying curled in soft rounded shape.
Slow look at dear one, dreaming
In his own small world - and
Wonder at those dreams that
Must be going through that little
Mind, causing swift flashes of
Smile on round small face.

Daughter pauses as she passes
Through room, loving smile at mother
And own tiny baby son, united
For once, not parted by all those
Dismal miles.

Turning page, looking up to
See a pair of sapphire blue eyes
Unblinking, solemnly regarding,
Assessing, maybe wondering who
That strange yet somehow familiar face
Belongs to. Then suddenly --
Recognition, acceptance. A happy
Smile breaks over the solemn little face
As grandma picks babe up out of chair
To hug and hold close, and both are
Suddenly enveloped in a burst of
Mutual love and happiness.

Oh! That moments such as these,
Could last forever...

D. C. S.

Parenthood

We're having a Baby! Isn't it grand
We're the happiest couple in all the land
When Baby is born we'll have people to tea
Just so they can say that Baby's like me.

But if Baby is crying, and bad tempered too
Then, darling **That Child** takes after you!

V. J. McTigue

A Mothers Love

A mother's love dawns
In the ecstasy of the first embrace
Obliterating any thoughts of pain.

A mother's love grows
In the warmth of the downy head at her breast,
The piano-playing fingers light against her skin,
The eyes, pools of innocence, wide with concentration,
Then shuttered in contentment.

A mother's love triumphs
When in greeting a winsome smile breaks forth.
When only she can comfort when in fret.
When, once clasping tightly, cries abate.

J. L. Smit

Birth Day

After pushing and pulling he enters
    the world
His legs are still bent and fingers
    are curled.
He lets out a cry - his lungs are
    all right
Dad cannot speak, his throat is
    too tight.
Mum asks the question, "Is
    everything there,
From his ten tiny toes to his
    fine downy hair?"
He's whisked off and washed,
    wrapped up in blue
Then he suckles the breast, knowing
    just what to do
Quickly he settles and closes his
    eyes
Contented and happy, he quietly
    sighs
Unaware of the pain, the love,
    the relief.
The incredible wonder,
    almost disbelief
That he's finally here and the
    joy of his birth
Is the sweetest, most precious
    event on God's earth.

Beverley Elliot

Bedtime

Once again I sit and wait while Tristan takes his time
Deciding he will have a play while mummy scribes a rhyme
I wrote a verse the other day, but now it's gone forever
I wrote it on the envelopes of cards for Derek and Heather.
Well anyway he's wide awake. Bedtime? Well it should be!
He's playing with his baby gym. A gymnast? Well he could be!
I should be tidying up and such while Dudley's still out working
Dinner to make and dishes to wash lest someone thinks I'm shirking
I'm not in what you'd call "poem mode"; this rhyme's not of my best
But at any rate I'm sitting down and getting a little rest
I've read it so far to Tristan here, he's lying there a' grinning
Thumping his feet 'gainst the carry cot, I think he thinks he's winning
But he's rubbing his eyes and slowing down, and "badva-ing" loud and
clear
And little does he know he'll soon be in bed, he's such a little dear
Now he's blowing raspberries and shouting to the skies
He's wrestling with the baby gym:- He's going to get a surprise ....
When suddenly I scoop him up to change his poo-ey nappy
I hope I hope he'll go to sleep so everyone will be happy
Oh dear oh dear it's getting worse I'm still struggling with this rhyme
I think I'm going to sort him out and tell him "It's your bedtime"!

Rosemary Wood

Child Of My Life

Miles is all smiles and
Smiles is all Miles.
       My beautiful child,
       My first born.
Miles is all smiles and
Miles is all mine
       My beautiful boy
       My first born child.

(M.A.S. 7.9.96)

Linda Santini

Roxanne

Holding you within my whole
You grew as did my heart,
Each tiny flutter of your caress
Made me realise the start
Of emotions new and gentle
Of tears and joy so sweet,
And with every day that passed
I longed for us to meet ....
To touch your tiny fingers
To look into your eyes
Knowing you are of me
From when I heard your cries.
Oh sweet and helpless baby
My life has just begun.
From the moment I conceived you
Our lives entwined as one.
Wrapped within this disbelief
My heart spins in a whirl,
And I thank whatever gods there are
For you my little girl.

LOVE MUMMY.
XXXXXXXXXX

V. Thompson

Christopher Says

I know that you love me so it's no surprise
That you're there in the moment I open my eyes
Pick me up promptly and if I'm not happy
Love me or feed me or check on my nappy
Wrap me all up in a shawl soft and warm
Keep me close by you and keep me from harm
Take me out shopping and spend all your money
'Cos I want a brand new activity bunny
Show me off daily, tell all of your joy
That you have a wonderful new baby boy
Dress me up smartly in my little clothes
But you'll give me a bath before that, I suppose
Give me that warm stuff that fills up my tummy
And cuddle me close 'till I fall asleep, Mummy!

D. Hickinbottom

Untitled

Two little girls of what joy
not that they wouldn't have
welcomed a boy
Just babies to cherish
to love and to hold
to teach all the good things
that life can behold
To guide them to know
the right from the wrong
and thank god for his
blessing all their lives long.

E. V. Benning

Baby Blues

Bouncing baby on my lap
(Can't you see my hair's gone flat?),
Changing nappies on the floor.
(Who's that calling at the door?),
A feed at 12, another at 2,
(Is there any chance I'll get to the loo?).
A trip in the car to soothe those cries
(Is it possible to eat and drive?)
She falls asleep within my arms
(Oh drat, there goes the car alarm!)
At last within the crib she lies,
(So peaceful that I miss those cries),
By now the time is half-past ten
(Time to sleep before she wakes again).

Catherine Bigland

Twins

Never a moment
    with two little boys
Plenty to tidy
    with twice the toys

Always fighting
    with two lots of tears
Competing for status
    but equal in years

Four little boots
    trailing in mud
Four dirty handprints
    ingrained in the wood

Different t.v. programmes
    both at the same time
Two favourite drinks
    one lemon, one lime

No chance of silence
    with twice the noise
Plenty of upsets
    but double the joys.

J. Chadwick

The Awakening

She sleeps,
I gaze down on her peaceful face.
Dark lashes touching rosy cheeks.
Her lips a perfect Cupid's bow,
Each breath as sweet as fairy cake.

She stirs,
I hold my breath and wait,
Her murmur, music, soft and light.
Pink fingers rub at sleepy eyes,
Which open wide, deep pools of blue.

She smiles,
I take her into my arms,
Body warm and soft as candy-floss.
Soft silky hair, her crown of gold,
My darling girl, my wish come true!

Lindsay Allen

Ours And Baby's View

Babies can be quite content,
Girgles, giggles, not absent.
Tummy full and nappy clean,
Makes their little faces gleam.

Lots of love and cuddles too,
And a game of peek a boo.
Many things to see and learn,
To venture out, they do yearn.

I can crawl, yip pee yip pee,
Get up to mischief, TE HE HE.
Climbing here and crawling there,
Mummy's pulling out her hair.

All I hear is no No NO!
That's the only word I know.

If I can not have my way,
Screaming on the floor, I'd stay.
Does not seem to do much good,
As my mum just stared and stood.

Babies are so cute and sweet,
From their heads down to their feet,
The best sized person you could meet,
With a smile that makes my day complete.

Jayne Sears

Untitled

I work a fifteen hour shift,
Nurturing life's precious gift,
And one question makes me quite berserk -
When will you go back to work?

For anyone who cares to hear,
I'd like to make things very clear
I do not relax, read or knit
I barely find the time to sit.

The cinema, the pub, what are they?
My life is filled with childish play
Some people give me a wide berth
While others think I'm Mother Earth,

Cooking, cleaning, washing, ironing
I find them all very trying.
A smile is sometimes hard to muster,
When life revolves around a duster.

Yet when I see your smiling face,
I know you are my saving grace.
Life will never be humdrum,
Now that I've become a mum.

Helen Stuart

Stephenie

As you were lying in our bed,
I gently kissed your soft sweet head,
I kissed your tummy and I kissed your toes
I gently kissed your tiny nose.

With eyes so blue and a smile so bright,
I held you close all through the night,
When you arrived so innocent and new,
A world of love you brought with you.

We thankyou Lord up above
For this child you gave us to love
Our precious gift to cherish and raise
Who will bring us joy in so many ways.

Cindy C. Devlin

The Precious Year

God gave us such a perfect gift
For one whole precious year,
A darling little blue-eyed girl
So innocent, so dear.

We didn't understand, you see,
That she was just a loan,
Until He called her back again
To His eternal home.

Now through life we journey on,
Hiding many a tear,
But from our hearts we say to Him,
"Oh, thank You for that year!"

J. M. Macsween

For Serené

Bouncy, bouncy, giggle, giggle.
On her changing mat,
She's ready to wriggle
Left or right;
Refusing her change,
Playing much better,
It's all one big game:

Banging and crashing,
Rolling around in her walker,
Moving one foot, then the other,
Laughing all the way;
She jolts into the sofa,
Stuck no-where to go.

She pushes and pushes,
Calling dada for help,
He encourages her to move forward,
Bribing her with some food,
But she still refuses to move;
Still stuck on the spot,
Screaming seems to be her answer,
Then he'll move her for sure.

After her dinner's gone down,
Off to the bouncer she goes,
Spinning and laughing,
Enjoying her own sounds.

She'll soon get tired,
So off to bed she goes,
Watching her mobile,
And with her teddy in hand,
Relaxed and contented, what a fun day she's had.

A. E. Bolton

Ode to Katie

On the second of December in nineteen ninety-five,
A friendly stork came knocking at our door.
"I've a little girl called Katie - she's really rather weighty
And my poor old beak's about to hit the floor!".

"Would you like to take her from me, coz I've got more work to do?
You look the sort of couple who'd be kind.
Your yellow lab called Sparkie and your daughter Caroline
Are both so nice, I'm sure they wouldn't mind!".

Before us lay this gorgeous babe with shock of jet black hair.
She really was a beauty to behold;
A piece of family treasure, a God-gift - made to measure,
For that same day Gran was eighty-three years old!

"Of course! We'd be delighted" we said in unison.
"We'd love to take her home and make her ours.
We'll re-locate the office and make a nurs'ry sweet,
With toys and books, balloons and hearts and flowers!".

So Katie came to live with us and now she's one year old,
She sits and rolls and crawls and smiles a lot!
We look on in total awe as her little life unfolds
And watch her sleeping quietly in her cot.

We thank you God, for sending her to comfort and console,
Each love-filled day exceeds the one before.
We're really very pleased that, after thirteen years,
A friendly stork came visiting us once more!

Paula Ryder

Will You Be

Will you be strong and will you be proud
Will you be honest and not afraid to speak out loud.

Will you be loyal, faithful and just
Will you be considerate and a man to trust.

Will you be kind, and will you be fair or
Will you be rebellious and grow long hair.

Will you be shy, sweet and demure or
Will you be brave, outgoing and sure.

Will you be tall, short, fat or thin
Whatever your stature you're going to win.

Will you love your Mother and Father
Or will these sentiments just be a palaver.

Will you be able to feel our love shining through
Whatever you will be, we'll always love you.

Jake, what will you be?

DEDICATED TO JAKE OLIVER MICHAELS, BORN 16TH
AUGUST 1995.

Jeremy D. Michaels

RHYMING SORROWS FROM THE HEART

by
Julie Richardson

My father died two years ago with cancer. I loved my father very much; he was my best friend as well as the best father anyone could have wished for. Since his death I have found it hard to grieve and I spent most of my time in my bedroom. But then something happened. I started to put my feelings down on paper and then I realised that not only was I crying, but the words that I wrote, were coming out in rhyme.

> I found that when I read my poems
> They made me cry.
> I read them time and time again,
> Until my tears run dry.
> Open your heart and cry,
> Don't hide them away inside.

You can place your order now
from all good bookstores

£2.99 - Softback   **ISBN 0 7223 3039 1**

**For each book sold, the author will
donate 10p from her royalty to Cancer Research**